HANDBOOK

FOR THE UPHEAVAL

TONY CARAVAN

LIVING IN FEUDAL AMERICA WITH CLIMATE CHANGE ENDLESS WARS, MILITARIZED POLICE, DOMESTIC SPYING, WAGE SLAVERY & CORPORATE GREED CAPITALISM

ISBN-13: 978-1514223772

ISBN-10: 1514223775

First Edition

ROCKFLUX : Filmworks : Music : Publishing — Rockflux.com

for someone like you

 **FORWARD**

EVERYTHING CHANGES

A Very Brief History of Death and Destruction by Nature and Man

Every year the Moon gets a couple of inches further away from the Earth. Actually, billions of years ago, the Moon was 10 times closer (bigger in the sky) than it is today. It affects our tides and the cycles of life.

Over time, the Earth has been bombarded by comets, meteors and asteroids. Scientists believe the Earth collided with a near planet-size object which formed the moon. Subsequently, our world has experienced mass extinctions and terraforming "sterilizations" that have reshaped the entire surface of the planet numerous times.

Many millions of years ago the days were shorter. And, at one point, there were over 400 days in a year due to the speed of the spin of the planet.

The north and south (magnetic) poles have shifted over time; meaning that every 200,000 years or so, a compass will point in the opposite direction.

The last Ice Age[1] ended approximately 11,000 years ago. About that time, civilizations started to pop up on the planet. However, there is evidence in the archaeological record that points to earlier settlements—especially in many coastal areas—that were flooded over when the ice melted. How far back these ancient civilizations go is still yet to be determined.

Species die off regularly, water levels rise and fall to create and eliminate shorelines, continents drift and quake and form mountain ranges, volcanoes spew out lava which piles up to make islands, and their dust blocks off the sunlight and cools the planet—even preventing plants and trees from growing, from time to time.

---

1 In previous Ice Ages parts of the United States were covered with glaciers over a mile thick. The last Ice Age (there have been five) began over two and half million years ago in the Pleistocene epoch, and started to thaw approximately 110,000 B.C.E. We are currently in what is called an interglacial period.

At any given moment this rock we live on is in a state of flux.

And if all that wasn't enough to show us how fragile our existence is; the corporate-industrialists over the last 150 years have, and continue to, destroy forests, pollute the water, fill the atmosphere with poisonous gases, create nuclear waste, dump toxic chemicals and materials into landfills (and the oceans), strip-mine the planet for minerals, and coerce governments to create armies to kill for strategic access to fossil fuels and other resources.

In 2015, we actually passed the "tipping point" with Carbon Dioxide (CO_2) rising to over 400 ppm[2], and we also experienced the warmest temperatures on record. And we now know that the current high levels of CO_2, the chief greenhouse gas in the atmosphere, are the result of human activities[3]. If we continue on this path, life as we know it will become unsustainable. There will be more violent storms and severe droughts, and more coastal areas will be flooded.

The most bizarre thing about man's part in these (recent) catastrophic "Earth changes," is the magnitude of death and destruction we have rained down on this planet in such a relatively short period of time.

Considering that another major city could be devastated by a severe hurricane, or that we could experience a major earthquake or tsunami—at any given moment; you'd think we'd cherish our time being alive, and appreciate the beauty of nature that surrounds us.

Instead, we allow corporations and politicians to enslave us with meaningless jobs that take up most of our waking hours—very few of which serve any real purpose for the betterment of the human condition, or the planet as a whole. Basically, life has become a work-eat-sleep existence for the accumulation of pieces of paper with dollar signs printed on them. All, so we can keep buying more disposable things, or spend our money on activities of diversion— further squandering our short existence.

Meanwhile, the infrastructure in the U.S. is crumbling. It is estimated that it would take trillions of dollars to repair and/or rebuild our bridges, railways, power grids and underground pipelines.

2 The consensus of climate scientists is that the upper safety limit for atmospheric CO2 is 350 parts per million (ppm). *Source: 350.org*

3 Over 97 percent of actively publishing climate scientists now agree that climate-warming trends over the past century are very likely due to human activities. *Source: NASA*

Our clean water supplies are dwindling; not necessarily due to the lack of fresh water (though climate change is creating serious droughts); but due to the mis-allocation of use, and waste by manufacturers that design products with a limited useful life (planned obsolescence), along with factory farms—that also pollute groundwater and streams with pesticides that have been linked to a dramatic increase in autism and the death of the honey bees.

The elderly in this country struggle to pay their household bills and their constantly rising medical costs. In fact, the quality of life for most average Americans keeps getting worse, year after year (no matter which political party is in power).

The pharmaceutical companies have priced many life saving drugs out of the financial means of many of the people who need them the most. In addition, they have lobbied to pass laws to prevent the importation of cheaper generic drugs (with the exact same ingredients—produced the exact same way) from being able to be sold here and abroad. One very tragic example of this was perhaps responsible for the deaths of over ten million Africans with AIDS[4], who were denied access to treatment that could improve their health, quality of life, and even prevent women from passing the disease on to their unborn children. At the same time, even in the U.S., patients were charged $15,000 a year for antiretroviral drugs that were available in India for only $100 a year, or 30 cents a day.

Our primary schools have become factories—designed to eliminate individuality and creativity, and to "program," distract and manipulate the young into conformity. A college education has become an over-priced commodity, that plunges people, just starting out, into extreme debt that they will carry with them for most of their adult lives—guaranteeing a life of servitude to their corporate-government masters—if they're lucky enough to even find a job.

It's almost as if mass insanity has infected the entire species. We've become a murderous race with delusions of grandeur, who believe we have a "God-given right" to rule over and enslave the poor and the weak. We're a bunch of overly-perfumed and ridiculously-frocked pack rats who collect shiny objects, drive and fly around in chunks of metal and plastic, and constantly compete to show we are better than those less fortunate than us.

---

4 *Source: Fire in the Blood* (2013 film), a documentary by Dylan Mohan Gray

We've paved over the Earth—building hives for the workers and monuments for the most corrupt and evil among us.

There are now well over seven billion people[5] breathing, eating and defecating all over the planet. There is bigotry, fighting, killing, oppression, starvation, disease, inequality and violent crimes being committed on every continent.

The so-called advanced nations survive (and flourish) by waging wars—mostly on the weaker underdeveloped nations. They fight, steal, spy, bully and intimidate to acquire natural resources and prime real estate.

Modern societies are built upon imaginary economies of paper money and digital credit ledgers in "the cloud"—most of which have no physical backing. 99 percent of the citizens live lives in pursuit of acquiring the financial means to just stay alive, pay tribute to the autocrats, and buy unnecessary things they are told they need. The populous has been seduced into believing that their leaders are good, warriors are heroes, and the more possessions they have, the happier they will be. Nothing could be further from the truth.

In this book I explore these and other topics of the day, but first permit me to share a few quotes from Mahatma Gandhi that I believe put much of this into perspective:

"An eye for an eye will only make the whole world blind."

"When I despair, I remember that all through history the way of truth and love have always won. There have been tyrants and murderers, and for a time, they can seem invincible, but in the end, they always fall. Think of it—always."

"What difference does it make to the dead, the orphans and the homeless, whether the mad destruction is wrought under the name of totalitarianism or in the holy name of liberty or democracy?"

"Earth provides enough to satisfy every man's needs, but not every man's greed.,"

"First they ignore you, then they ridicule you, then they fight you, and then you win."

—Tony Caravan
Summer 2015

---

5 It is projected that in 30 years the global population may increase to over nine billion people. *Source: U.S. Census Bureau*

"AN EYE FOR AN EYE WILL ONLY MAKE THE WHOLE WORLD BLIND."

—Mahatma Gandhi

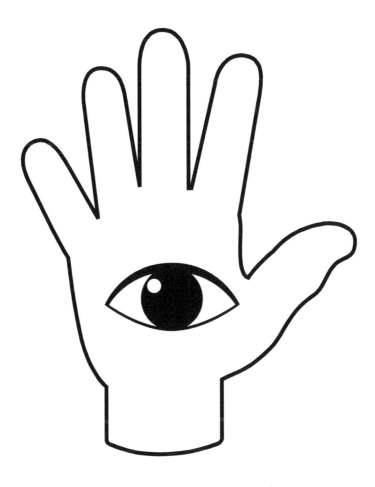

Hamsa symbol - Hebrew: הַסְמַה believed to provide defense against the evil eye

Chapter hand numerals are based on ASL, or American Sign Language, invented by Laurent Clerc and Thomas Hopkins Gallaudet in 1817, with kudos to Abbe Charles Michel de L'Epee inventors of French Sign Language in 1771 and Martha's Vineyard Sign Language (MVSL) in the 17th century.

CONTENTS

HANDBOOK FOR THE UPHEAVAL

*A collection of mostly essays
with cut-outs for posting and printing.*

TONY CARAVAN

THE ONE PERCENT DEPENDS ON YOUR SERVITUDE AND OBEDIENCE

Something that's not aired on the nightly newscasts, or written about in the mainstream press and blogs is how dependent the rich actually are on the poor.

From the very beginning, those in power have increased their material wealth, stature and land holdings on the backs of their fellow human beings (or, the 99 percent).

In most cases, like the first several hundred years in The Americas, it was through direct slavery[1] and theft. A fact that, to this day, is downplayed in schools and dramatic re-tellings of history. Many of the most powerful corporations and financial firms, that still survive today (in one way, shape or form), derived their profusion of opulence by stealing land from indigenous peoples, raping and slaughtering millions of people, stealing all of their worldly possessions, and then putting the survivors to work for them.

In the case of the U.S., we not only did all of that to the native Americans; but we also rounded up people in Africa—breaking up families and uprooting entire cultures—put them in chains, stuffed them in boats, sold them, and sent them to forced-labor camps called plantations. This is how America was built, on the backs of slaves.

But enough on that unbelievable and horrific founding of this country; let's move forward in history...

The same "power elite" now needed workers for their industrial factories, farms and railroads. So they "employed" men, women and children on 12-hour or longer shifts—6 days a week—with unsafe working conditions, and paid them meager wages that were barely enough to buy a few rags to wear, and the basic foods to keep their bodies strong enough to make it through another working week.

Meanwhile these "captains of industry" lived liked kings on great estates in mansions with furnishings, food and clothing beyond most workers wildest imaginations.

---

1 Howard Zinn, *A People's History of the United States* (HarperCollins, 1980) ISBN-13: 858-1000011323

And rather than despise these "robber barons," people admired them, looked up to them, and wanted to be like them. A fairy tale like *Cinderella²*, is an example of the foolish hopes and dreams that many of the working poor had to cope with their hopeless situation.

Others, of course, formed unions and managed to get child labor laws passed and reduce the work day to 12, 10, then eight hours—Monday through Friday. Which is still a bit absurd, if you think about it—that the majority of your waking hours are spent in servitude to people and companies that pay wages and salaries that are hardly enough to maintain a roof over your head and have enough to eat to work another week. —*I know, it sounds familiar, doesn't it?*

There are two take-aways from this:

First, that the people at the top, the so-called one-percenters, are not noble, special, better or anything even close to that. In fact, they are quite the very opposite. They are people, and descendants of people, who stole, tortured, schemed, and enslaved other people to get what they have. They are not to be envied or looked up to; on the contrary, many of them should be fined or imprisoned*!*

Second, the one-percenters need you in order to maintain their wealth and power. They make billions of dollars in profits on the sales of over-priced soft drinks, fast-foods, cars, insurance, alcohol, smartphones, TVs, loans, utilities and services. It's the exorbitant prices we pay to wear their brand names that keeps them in business.

Remember that "we the people" have the right to "life, liberty and the pursuit of happiness." We also have the right to organize, protest and strike. We can demand a "living wage," better health care and retirement benefits; and even longer vacation times and shorter work weeks. We do not have to give the majority of our waking life in servitude to these people—just because this is the way it's always been—or because they dress better and have way bigger houses.

Think about why the divide between the rich and poor is so great. We're talking billionaires versus people making only tens of thousands of dollars. That gap alone, demonstrates that there is plenty of flexibility within the corporate structure to make concessions for the people who make the lifestyles of the rich and famous possible.

2 Jacob and Wilhelm Grimm, *"Aschenputtel," Kinderund Hausmärchen*
[Children's and Household Tales -- Grimms' Fairy Tales], 7th edition
(Göttingen: Verlag der Dieterichschen Buchhandlung, 1857), no. 21, pp. 119-26

THE MAJORITY OF YOUR WAKING HOURS ARE SPENT IN SERVITUDE

Now I realize that you may be content right now with your smartphone, Facebook, Netflix, iTunes, frappuccino, and WiFi-enabled car; but how long do you think you'll be able to afford all of those diversions from reality? It's just a matter of time before the price of gas goes up again, food and drink prices increase, taxes rise, rents go up, interest rates rise, utility fees spike, etc., etc... On top of that, our infrastructure is crumbling, there's a looming shortage of clean water, climate change is real, and all the wars we're fighting now, will ultimately come back to bite us—just like they did before.

If there's any hope for a better future, it's through spreading the word that "the emperor isn't wearing any clothes.[3]" Publicly criticize the rich—call them out on their lies and wrongdoings, stop worshipping their "cult of personality," and for cryin' out loud, don't support the two party political system—Democrats and Republicans are two sides of the same coin—especially when it comes to following the commands of the corporate lobbyists.

We don't need better political leaders, we need better movements by the people.

As Bob Marley[4] sang, it's time to:

"Get up, stand up: stand up for your rights!
Get up, stand up: don't give up the fight!"

---

3 Hans Christian Andersen, *The Emperor's New Clothes* (C. A. Reitzel, Copenhagen, 1837)

4 Bob Marley, Peter Tosh, *Get Up, Stand Up*, Copyright: Embassy Music Corporation, BMG Rights Management (Ireland) Ltd.

OCCUPY EVERYWHERE!

"Occupy Everywhere" was written on a cardboard sign(s) seen during the Occupy Wall Street movement in New York City (and elsewhere). It was also part of the title of a documentary directed by Michael Perlman, The 99%: Occupy Everywhere.

HANDBOOK

DO WE REALLY LIVE IN A DEMOCRACY?

How Much Freedom Do We Really Have?

Those are the types of questions that if you ask them, people look at you like you should be hauled away in a straight jacket. But after their initial knee-jerk reaction, the brave ones realize that these are perhaps very important questions to ask. In fact, considering how much the words democracy and freedom are thrown around these days; and how people go to war and die or lose limbs in the belief that they are protecting these liberties, I'd say they may be two of the most important questions of our time.

First let's look at democracy... As Professor Richard D. Wolff points out in his book, *Democracy at Work: A Cure For Capitalism*[1], most of us spend five out of seven days a week—the best hours of the day—working for a company that does not abide by the rules of democracy. In other words, most workplaces are totalitarian in nature and you do not participate in any major decision making about the business, the products or services produced, how much you are paid, etc.

You may argue that of course a business is not a democracy, it's a business; but that would be missing the point. If most of your day is spent at a place that is not a democracy, and you sleep for another third of the day, that means that for two-thirds of the day you are technically not living in a democracy. *But it gets worse...*

So what do we do with the remaining third of our day? Most people rush around to take care of family matters and household responsibilities; or, if they are lucky, they get to spend some time taking part in some sort of leisure activity or diversion like watching TV, a movie or a sporting event. In most of these pastimes we do not participate either; rather, we observe, and are encouraged to buy products from the sponsors. —Not a very democratic activity either.

In fact, unless you participate in a community organization or some sort of social group or committee, you rarely see democracy in action.

---

1 Richard Wolff, *Democracy at Work: A Cure For Capitalism* (Haymarket Books, 2012) ISBN-13 9781608462476.

Of course, there are elections, right? *Well, let's look at those...* Think about who chooses the candidates in the first place. Usually it's some group or organization, or a member of an extremely wealthy family that decides to (or is chosen to) run. The average American has very little to do with the selection of candidates (except for an occasional independent nominee). Then, corporations and political action committees (PACs) finance the campaigns—spending millions of dollars on advertising. The media, being the recipient of those millions of dollars, gives airtime to these mainstream candidates to make sure they keep the political revenue stream coming in from future Democrats and Republicans. Ultimately, when the candidates get elected, they are beholden to their corporate donors (and lobbyists) who write the laws and tell them how to vote. Again, not so democratic as we are led to believe.

It is also worth noting how the media functions after the election. On major issues, the press will act as public relations agents for the politicians; and report (or not report) stories as they are instructed to do so. When asked why, most honest reporters will explain it is to keep their access to their contacts in government. Something most elected officials use (and abuse) to their advantage on the big issues.

Now let's look at freedom... Freedom and democracy pretty much go hand-in-hand. And so it follows that you rarely experience freedom at the workplace; and since sleep doesn't count, we're back to that two-thirds of your life being spent not being truly free either. As for the remaining one third, or "free time," I wouldn't exactly call that very free either. No doubt, we are free-er than the Chinese and many other foreign nationals. But the question here is not whether we are free-er; it's rather, are we truly free?

Personally, I wouldn't call what we have true freedom. Almost every aspect of our lives is regulated, controlled or guided by a set of rules. We need licenses, degrees and approvals. We have to fill out forms, pay fees, taxes, insurance and tolls. Our land can be taken away by eminent domain, our driving privileges can be revoked, we can't even drink a beer on our own porch in many states. If a whistle-blower tries to practice free speech, he or she is fired, intimidated and/or arrested. The government and corporations spy on us daily, and keep files on everything we do—in the name of national security or to better market their products to us, respectively. People are restricted from protesting or assembling in public—even with a permit. *—And the list goes on...*

Oh, sure, we have some freedoms, but they're hardly what they're touted to be. Meaning that those wars we fight to protect our so called freedom don't make a helluva-lot of sense when you start counting or trying to make a list.

Usually by this point, there are people who get so befuddled that they say, "if you don't like it here, why don't you leave?" At which I usually respond by laughing and saying, "did you listen to anything I said? You are proving my point!"

The idea of living in a democracy is that you have a right to your opinion, a right to be heard, and what you say should matter and be counted—whether it's a majority or a minority viewpoint. Those who love to throw around the words democracy and freedom the most, are usually the ones who tend to restrict or want to take them away from us.

THOSE WHO LOVE TO THROW AROUND THE WORDS DEMOCRACY AND FREEDOM THE MOST, ARE USUALLY THE ONES WHO RESTRICT THEM OR WANT TO TAKE THEM AWAY FROM US.

IT'S TIME TO DO THE RIGHT THING

"The medium is the message." —Marshall McLuhan

We all get diverted from reality every now and then—some more than others. But it's not our fault that our lives have become a merry-go-round of work-eat-sleep-play a little, work-eat-sleep-shop, work-eat-sleep-worry, etc... We're so consumed with surviving and trying to find a few moments to feel like a human being, that we lose touch with what's going on around us.

In our moments of clarity, we know that the one percenters are screwing us over. We know that the politicians are doing the bidding of their corporate puppet-masters. We know that the fossil fuel industry is threatening our future existence on this planet; and we know that there are too many wars, there is too much hatred, and not enough compassion. And without a doubt, the "cost of living" is way too high for the wages most people earn. We know about all of those things and many more injustices here and around the world. But we're busy, we're tired, and sometimes we just want to escape from all of the madness and just have a few drinks with some friends, get lost in our apps, or just pretend that the outside world doesn't exist.

There's nothing wrong with that. It's not our fault that we have to work most of our waking hours to pay our bills. It's not our fault that we don't have universal (free) health care. It's not our fault that politicians break their promises with smiles and well-crafted emotional speeches that fool us into believing that they will change things. It's also not our fault that the fossil fuel industry is polluting the air, water and land. And it's not our fault that the Wall Street-ers spend billions to change the laws in their favor. None of these things are our fault.

But that was yesterday...

If we're going to salvage all that is good about this civilization we have, we need to find the time to start making a difference today.

It can start with a tweet or a re-tweet, a conversation with a friend or a stranger where you let them know the truth behind the lies. It means giving some time, a signature, or even just one dollar to a worthy cause. If a million people gave a dollar to support something, or signed a petition, that's a million dollars or a million signatures that can't be ignored.

I've decided to start divesting myself from everything that is negative in this world. I'm starting today; and I hope you join me, and the millions of others who are already bravely standing up for what's right, what is good, and what is necessary.

As Victor Laslo said in *Casablanca*[1], "Welcome back to the fight. This time I know our side will win."

---

1 *Casablanca* (© Warner Bros. 1942 film) Directed by Michael Curtiz

DIVEST!

THE ABSURDITY OF POLARITY

"The only difference between the Republican and Democratic parties is the velocities with which their knees hit the floor when corporations knock on their door. That's the only difference."

—Ralph Nader

The taking of sides has led to the downfall of civilizations from the earliest times. This genetically inherited idea of positive and negative, good versus evil, and us versus them is destroying us.

If there is any purpose for the modern human brain's existence, it is to think creatively and have the insight to solve problems in extraordinary ways. This is what sets us apart from all of the other living things (at least the ones that we know of).

The biggest obstacle for mankind (and this planet) is polarity. East versus West, Democrats versus Republicans, Capitalists versus Socialists, Environmentalists versus Energy Companies, Science versus Religion, Black versus White, Rich versus Poor, etc., etc...

We are so consumed with defending and fighting for "our side's" cause, that we demean, hate, hurt and even kill in the name of our chosen ideals or beliefs. This has become so ingrained in our social structures, that we've lost sight of what is true and what is real. We have closed our minds to arguments that may disprove our core beliefs, for so long, that the very reasons for our endless struggles with our perceived enemies are baseless, or questionable at best.

We think we know the truth, but in reality, there is very little that we know to be absolutely true. Most of what we know has been passed down through generations, the educational system, and now the electronic media. The idea that our heroes or the attractive person on TV or YouTube might be wrong, is not open for debate.

But what if nobody is right, and nobody is wrong? What if the difficulties that we wrestle with each day just went away? What if both "sides" decided to live and let live. What if we all worked to improve the human condition as a whole?

It's called peace. It's almost a bad word, or cowardly word in today's mainstream culture. We've been at each other's throats for so long now, that we only see the violent acts we perform against one another; and neither side has a goal for after the fighting ends?

Winning, that's the goal, right? Colonialism, empire, conversion, rule, control, laws and imprisonment. That's what happens to the conquered. Then their relatives, countrymen, followers, start the whole fighting over again for revenge and to conquer and rule over those who enslaved them. It's an endless war for power, land, resources—whatever; and it produces endless death and destruction throughout the world.

If we'd only use our creative brains to reason our way out of this cycle of violence and hatred. Because, the truth is, everyone's "end game" is exactly the same. Humans want love, warmth, companionship, a place to live without the threat of being harmed, food to eat, clean water to drink, protection from the weather, families, children and to be happy. And no person that believes in love and happiness should accept the harming or killing of another person to achieve that. *It's absurd!*

My humble advice to all of the haters and fighters is to contemplate why you are doing what you are doing. And don't say for freedom and country—those are intangibles created by propagandists to keep you at odds with others. Think about what your personal end game is. What will make your life happy?

If we all had happiness as a goal, the polarity would be defeated. The only true enemy in the world is hatred. Eliminate hate, and we all win.

Now, though I'd like to end there, the reality is, that there are mentally ill people out there, who want to harm other people, for the sake of harming people. We must restrain them, treat them (if possible), but not use them as an excuse to hate or harm everyone who looks like them, or comes from the same place as they do, or has the same religion, culture or politics.

Just as the fish live in the sea, the birds fly in the sky, and live in the trees, and the insects crawl on the ground, we should have the common sense to take a lesson from nature, and find our place on this planet, and let others have their place.

By no means is any of this an easy task. But the reason it is possible (peace, that is), is because deep down inside people want it.

The true enemies of the people, are the people who polarize us, and profit on it. If we ignore the political parties, and taking sides on issues, and encourage those in power to work for our basic human needs and wants, we can make this a better world, and it would be a way better use of our ginormous brains.

THE TRUE ENEMIES OF THE PEOPLE, ARE THE PEOPLE WHO POLARIZE US, AND PROFIT ON IT.

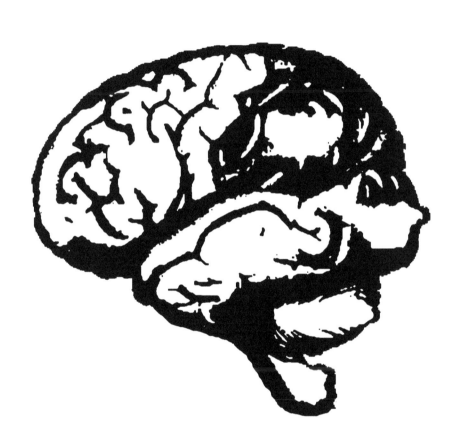

WHAT A WASTE OF TIME

One of the primary things that separates human beings from the rest of the animals roaming about this planet are our oversized brains. That, and the fact that we're the only species that kill each other for ideological reasons. It reminds me of that line in that Thompson Twins song[1], *"Well, Cleopatra died for Egypt, what a waste of time."*

At this juncture, considering all of the accumulated knowledge and technologies produced by mankind's greatest minds over the millennia, we should be accomplishing fantastic things beyond the scope of our current comprehension. But instead we're puttering along in the natural and social sciences and the humanities.

Now before you get too bent out of shape, I'm talking about breakthroughs like Jonas Salk's polio vaccine or Louis Pasteur's germ theory—which not only improved the human condition, but were given freely to all mankind (without some pharmaceutical company holding the patent).

To be sure, in recent years, there have been notable major advancements such as human genome sequencing, the CERN Large Hadron Collider, the smart-phone, planetary science discoveries, robotics and cloning. But when it comes improving the quality of life for the average inhabitant of this planet, we're proceeding at a snail's pace. *I mean things like alleviating poverty, disease and providing access to clean water and shelter.*

Hell, we still haven't cured cancer and most of the other deadly diseases. We depend too heavily on fossil fuels to power practically everything we use (at the expense of destroying the planet). Our buildings roads and bridges don't last very long, and neither do our automobiles, appliances and machines. And I'm sure you can think of dozens of more things that could (and should) be much better.

---

1 "Lies" performed by the Thompson Twins, written by Crandall Jr, William / Charles, Beau © Sony/ATV Music Publishing LLC, Warner/Chappell Music, Inc., Kobalt Music Publishing Ltd., Universal Music Publishing Group, O/B/O APRA AMCOS

The reason that things haven't improved for most people over the last 50 years is simple: we've been too preoccupied with entertaining and killing each other.

Think about it… the greatest advancements in recent decades have come in the areas of military weaponry, entertainment and gaming technologies. I mean—make no mistake about it—I think the smart-phone is an incredible device! But look how most people use it: tweeting, posting and sharing selfies all day long. And, while there's nothing wrong with that (most of us do it), it consumes far too much of our collective time, and employs far too many of our greatest minds. Time and people that could be solving real problems.

But let's forget about social media for a moment, and look at the single largest preoccupation of the 21st Century: WAR! We spend billions of dollars a day on killing machines (both mechanical and corporeal). And most of the time, it's like sticking a pole into a hornet's nest—every time there is "collateral damage," a whole new generation of revenge-seekers are created, and the cycle of violence starts all over again.

Look, I'm not naive or saying that there aren't wackos out there that would do us all harm, what I'm saying is that we need to find new and better ways to deal with the problems of the world.

And that brings us back to the premise of this article—we should be using our brains (not brawn) to find better solutions. If we focused the best minds to create extraordinary ways to end wars and violence, and improve the quality of life, then it wouldn't be a waste of time.

Perhaps the biggest missed opportunity of the last decade was when Barack Obama stood before the Nobel Peace Committee and said, "force can be justified" and "war is sometimes necessary." With the war-weary eyes and ears of the world focused on one man, instead of offering the prospect of peace, and an attempt to diffuse the conflicts in the Middle East and around the world, he chose to justify war and violence. It is quite possible that this was a defining moment in history that set us back a hundred years.

You see, the problem with the current system of militarization is that there is no end game. So each year there is more and more violence, despite all of the bullets and bombs used to quell it. President Obama was wrong when he said, "the instruments of war do have a role to play in preserving the peace." Killing only exacerbates the problems that caused the conflict in the first place.

Most people end up being in one of two camps on this: those who embrace the endless wars and violence (and profit on it); and those who ignore it completely, and divert themselves from the reality through entertainment. Meanwhile, the root problems are ignored, and our species gets closer and closer to self-annihilation.

I'd like to think that there are still people out there who believe that a better world is possible—and dream of a future without war, disease, poverty and all that nasty stuff. But until our greatest minds re-focus their efforts on solutions for humanity's problems, I'm afraid that this country will continue to be a giant amusement park that is funded by the death and destruction of others.

THE SINGLE LARGEST PREOCCUPATION OF THE 21ST CENTURY IS WAR!

Bikini Atoll Hydrogen Bomb "Test Baker" in 1946

THINGS YOU CAN DO WITH A HALF TRILLION DOLLARS

"Every gun that is made, every warship launched, every rocket fired signifies in the final sense, a theft from those who hunger and are not fed, those who are cold and are not clothed." — Dwight D. Eisenhower

The U.S. Defense Department's 2016 budget was $534 billion for military spending. Yes, that's right, over a half trillion, yes TRILLION DOLLARS, to destroy, kill and genuinely piss off foreigners. In effect, the government is tormenting an injured, wild animal, and all of us end up suffering the consequences. By the Pentagon's constant meddling in places that represent no "clear and present danger" to U.S. citizens, they are, in effect, putting U.S. citizens in harm's way. The complete opposite of their mission to "defend," or their cookie-cutter excuse of "national security."

Personally I believe they should rename the Defense Department back to the War Department[1] the way it was for over 150 years.

Most people don't see the tragedy and absurdity of what the military and their hired mercenaries and drones are doing. The propaganda machine (the media and pop culture) have twisted and warped and fabricated so many lies, that the average person believes the military is actually "a force for good in the world." Well, of course, nothing could be farther from the truth. There hasn't ever been this much violence and hatred in the world. It's everywhere, on every continent—and always nearby our "military activities."

It's very difficult to argue this issue, because the people who support the military, think like sports fans—they just cheer and "rah, rah" their team on to victory. When you ask them what victory is, they say freedom. But when you look around, every year we have less and less, so called, freedoms because of the actions of the military. *So, let's face it, it's a failed campaign for freedom!*

Now, on the other hand, we could take that HALF TRILLION DOLLARS and make sure our grandparents, parents and children

---

1 The War Department existed from 1789 until September 18, 1947, when it split into Department of the Army and Department of the Air Force and joined the Department of the Navy as part of the new joint National Military Establishment (NME), renamed the United States Department of Defense in 1949.
Source: Wikipedia

have enough to eat and access to health care and housing. We could fix all of the broken down things in this country that are making life miserable for the hard-working taxpayers who are the heart and soul of this decaying democracy. This would also create millions of jobs.

As for the military, they should be given a budget with enough to patrol our borders and "provide for the common defense." We need to get out of places we don't own or have any business being in. We should use our diplomatic corps to broker peace everywhere we've started wars; instead of using our embassies as spy stations for the war machine.

Deep down inside, all sane people want peace. Even the wackos out there waving flags and guns. They have family, children, homes and towns. The bottom line is, if we'd take the lead by being compassionate to our own people here at home, and stop messing with people and cultures we don't understand, we might start "winning the hearts and minds" of people around the world.

It's a very sad commentary on 21st Century life, but all of those destroyed villages, all of those hundreds of thousands of dead people, all of those broken and crippled bodies (both here at home and abroad) were for nothing.

If you need an example, look at what happened in Iraq. After thousands of U.S. soldiers gave their lives and limbs to "liberate" that country, all it did was lay the foundation for sectarian violence and the rise of the Islamic State and their wave of death and destruction.

Here at home, the average American is worse off than they were a decade ago; and, a decade ago, they were worse off than they were a decade before that. Forget about the war on terrorism, more people die from car crashes and suicide each year, than have died from terrorism over the entire term of the "war." *Let me say that again,* there are more people dying here at home from curable diseases, negligence in manufacturing, lack of proper nutrition, and domestic crimes and violence than all of the terrorist acts combined worldwide over the entire course of the War on Terror. *See the chart at right: causes of death in the U.S.*

Our primary focus should be on our people, and our country; and getting our house in order. Next, we should look at the rest of the world, and share our discoveries and promote peace.

Don't be fooled by the talking heads on TV, or characters in the war movies; war is not heroic, "war is hell." People die in war, both the paid soldiers and people caught in the cross-fire. The results of "undeclared wars" usually are only beneficial to some corporation that has an "interest" in the place where the battle is being fought (like oil or oil pipelines), or the military contractors who profit in the billions from the war itself.

A HALF TRILLION DOLLARS!!! Imagine the good we could do with A HALF TRILLION DOLLARS...!?!

Peace!

Causes of Death in the U.S.

Cause	Annual	*10 years
Heart disease:	611,105	6,100,000
Cancer:	584,881	5,800,000
Chronic lower respiratory diseases:	149,205	1,400,000
Accidents (unintentional injuries):	130,557	1,300,000
Stroke (cerebrovascular diseases):	128,978	1,200,000
Accidents[2]:	126,438	1,200,000
Alzheimer's disease:	84,767	840,000
Diabetes:	75,578	750,000
Influenza and Pneumonia:	56,979	560,000
Nephritis, nephrotic synd. & nephrosis:	47,112	470,000
Intentional self-harm (suicide):	41,149	410,000
Homicides:	16,121	160,000
Terrorism (includes 9/11 & Boston):	-	3,000

* Estimated over a decade at the current death rates
Disease and homicide statistics from CDC.gov (2015)

---

2 Accidents: Motor vehicle accidents, other land transport accidents, water, air and space accidents, accidental discharge of firearms, accidental drowning and submersion, falls, accidental exposure to smoke, fire and flames, accidental poisoning and exposure to noxious substances. *Source: MediLexicon*

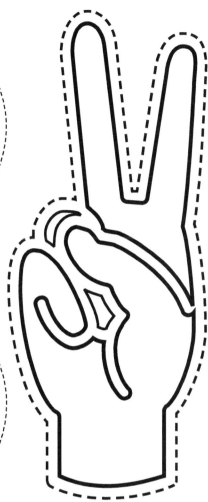

# WE'VE GOT SOME BIG PROBLEMS IN THIS COUNTRY

Yeah, I know, that's the understatement of the year... But what I'm referring to here are the tens of millions of unemployed, under-employed, under-paid, abused, mistreated, and the people who resort to selling drugs, contraband or committing crimes to make a living. Throngs of people in every city with basically nothing to do but eventually get in trouble. Now add to that the innocent people who get caught in the firing line of a militarized police force under a mandate by their corporate-backed city councils to keep "law and order" at any cost.

Quick observation: It's interesting to note how the police mission "to protect and serve" or to be "peace officers" has now been over-shadowed by the term, "law enforcement."

Looking at the riots in the streets that have taken place across the country, it seem that in many cities, both the cops and the "citizens" appear to be at their breaking points. And whether or not there are prosecutions of police or not, there is an undercurrent of distrust of people in authority by the poor and many of the working poor.

And, of course, it only gets worse each year—especially when the weather gets warmer, and people spend most of their time outdoors. When the kids are out of school in the summertime, and the gang[1] "busy season" begins, it's almost like a war zone in many places all across the U.S.[2]

This country also has a serious racial-profiling problem, with too many cops that view people of color as the enemy, not citizens to "protect and serve." Part of the cause of this unfortunate mentality is because there are too many ex-soldiers on police forces who haven't had the chance to be properly re-integrated into society. You can't just go from being trained to shoot to kill, and then given a gun and automatically become a "peace officer."

---

1 There are an estimated 850,000 gang members in the U.S. responsible for an estimated 13 percent of all homicides. *Source: NationalGangCenter.gov / FBI*

2 There are over 2 million emergency visits each year for assault in the U.S. *Source: CDC.org*

But that's only part of the story... We also have a culture that puts heavy demands on its citizens to buy and consume. And as the cost of living continues to rise, people become more and more frustrated that they cannot be an active participant in the good life they see portrayed on TV and in the movies. This creates resentment, jealousy—even anger. Add that to the general disenchantment with their struggle to survive, and you've got a tinderbox ready to ignite.

So what to do? More cops, more laws and curfews? More arrests? What then? Politicians stand on their soap boxes and offer the same solutions we've been hearing about for decades—most of which have only made the situation worse. Let's face it, things are starting to spin out of control.

Well, there are a number of solutions that can be implemented in a matter of weeks or months that could stop, reverse and eventually improve the situation nationwide. I've listed several below, but I'm sure you have one or two of your own to add.

1) People need to have something to do with their time. Whether it's a job, a project, volunteer work, something creative—whatever. The unemployed have too much idle time on their hands, coupled with no money—which is a very dangerous combination.

I propose that we solve this problem on the local level. Instead of building more office buildings and giving raises to bureaucrats and elected officials, or buying new city vehicles or surplus military assault weapons for the police; we need to create a jobs fund.

Here's how this would work...

People are paid $15/hour cash (less taxes, of course) to do various work around the city and in their neighborhoods. Jobs would range from cleaning and fixing to painting and planting. It could even involve creative arts projects like some of the old "New Deal" programs. The key is that you get paid cash for a day's work, and you get paid at the end of the day.

What this does is to gradually get people to want to go back into the workforce. Sure, some will work a day, then drink a day; but by equating a day's labor with a decent day's wage, eventually more and more time will be spent working than not. Plus, the community benefits greatly at the same time.

This program goes hand in hand with a minimum "living wage" law nationwide, so that people don't have to have two or three jobs to pay their bills. Companies also need to step up and address the inequality in corporate salaries and bonuses versus the wages of their workers.

Aside: In an ideal world, we would adopt the ideas of Jacque Fresco's[3] resource-based economy; but unfortunately, I don't believe people are ready for that yet.

2) We all have to admit that there is a serious racial problem in this country. And, that despite all of the progress that the civil rights movement has had on changing laws, there are still far too many racial inequalities, and way too many racists getting away with prejudice in the workplace, and violence and murder in the streets. We need to have a national dialogue on racism, and come to terms with this deadly problem. One would have thought this would have occurred during the Obama administration; but unfortunately, under his watch, the situation only got worse.

We have to find a way to live together without all of the hate. People of all backgrounds must to be involved—bigotry in many cases is a two-way street. We have to acknowledge and identify the root causes and start dealing with them directly. We must make changes in our communities that <u>go beyond passing laws</u>, but rather lay out blueprints for moving forward. The media, schools, government and organizations must get involved. This has to happen now, and it has to happen on the local level—right down to the neighborhoods.

3) We need to end the "War on Drugs" and admit that it was a failure. There needs to be an immediate review of the non-violent drug users in prison, and they should be released under the condition that they get treatment for their addiction.

In addition, there should be serious consideration of legalizing drugs to get them out of the hands of the drug cartels and gangs. There is too much money going into the hands of these criminals, and too much violence on the streets because of drug activities.

---

3 Jacque Fresco (born March 13, 1916), an American futurist and social engineer. Architect of The Venus Project, a system where financial influence and control would be eliminated.

Drugs should be legalized and taxed, and the taxes used to fund treatment programs throughout the country. Ralph Nader has presented some good ideas about this.

4) It's time once and for all to have universal free health care. And make sure that Social Security really covers the cost of living for seniors and those with disabilities. The idea that a person can't pay their basic bills on Social Security; and that Medicare is deducted from their check is unconscionable.

By now everyone has heard about Canada and European countries providing health care for their citizens. Critics need to be told that a system like Medicare for all would actually save the government money.

5) We need to aggressively embrace renewable energy sources such as solar power as a replacement to fossil fuels.

What most people don't realize is that practically every home in America can benefit from solar power in some way. Though obviously the southern states have an advantage over the north with the magnitude of sunlight available year round; even northern areas receive enough light to lower energy costs (and overall demand).

For those who don't know how solar works, it's like this:

When you use solar power, you're actually getting your electricity from stored battery power. The solar panels are used to charge your batteries, then a power inverter converts the battery (DC current) into usable AC, or household current, that you then simply "plug in" to.

Technically speaking, it takes about a half dozen solar panels several hours to charge a 200 amp, 12V battery. However, you can "trickle-charge" a battery with a single solar panel over a longer period of time. The number of panels and batteries you need depends on how many watts of power you use. The formula (for the geeks out there) is watts = volts x amps.[4]

Depending on your individual electrical needs, you can set up a solar power system just for lighting (usually self-contained units), or a multi-panel system to run a specific appliance or an entire house (the number of panels is based on wattage).

---

4 Source: GreatSolarStuff.com

Most solar installations can be completed in a day or two. Prices range from hundreds to thousands of dollars, depending on the amount of power you need. However, with tax rebates and incentives, those prices can be cut dramatically. And with most systems lasting up to 20 years or more, it's very cost-effective to add solar into your electric mix.

These are just a few ideas of how to start dealing with some of the problems we face; and yes, some of them deal with programs that cost money. But in a country where nearly half of our national budget goes to the military, surely we can shave off a few billion here and there to take care of the well being of our people. After all, it's our (tax) money—we should have a say in how it's spent!

If we rise above politics, greed, jealousy and hate, we can solve all of the important issues of the day. If we don't, you don't need me to tell you, that the outlook is bleak.

WE NEED TO END THE "WAR ON DRUGS" AND ADMIT THAT IT WAS A FAILURE.

NON-VIOLENT DRUG USERS IN PRISON SHOULD BE RELEASED AND TREATED FOR ADDICTION.

"MOST PEOPLE FORGET THAT IN A DEMOCRACY, THERE ARE NO 'LEADERS,' ONLY REPRESENTATIVES OF THE PEOPLE.

STEALING, SPYING, TORTURING & KILLING FOR WHAT?

"The U.S. National Security Agency has figured out how to hide spying software deep within hard drives, giving the agency the means to eavesdrop on the majority of the world's computers, according to cyber researchers and former operatives..."— Reuters (2015)

With the recent passage of the "USA Freedom Act," after several surveillance-related provisions in the PATRIOT Act where allowed to expire; many privacy advocates, led by Senator Rand Paul (R-KY), felt they had achieve a victory in Congress, and vowed to continue the fight with future amendments. And while any reform to the NSA's sweeping powers of intrusion into American's private lives is a good thing, don't start feeling warm and fuzzy just yet.

As we have learned from the media reports on the revelations by Edward Snowden, Chelsea Manning and through WikiLeaks and others, there is far more going on in secret (behind the scenes) than most people could possibly imagine. After all, the so called, "intelligence" agencies (both the ones we know about, and the ones who's existence is hidden) are in the secrecy business. Basically, these people lie for a living; which has played out time and again at Congressional hearings and in statements to the press. What most people don't realize is that most of the secrets that are classified under "national security" are really protecting corporate security, and hiding the underhand, and mostly illegal activities, being done with taxpayer dollars around the world (and here in our own country).

By now we all know about the torture and private prisons and secret executions, but what we don't hear much about are the cases of computer hacking and manipulation of global markets to benefit the financial industry and corporations that run Congress.

And when most people see violence erupting everywhere around the world, they see it in terms of "us versus them," not as cause and effect with layers beneath the surface and a means of creating revenue streams for war profiteers (the military contractors).

Maybe it's time we demand that Congress takes a deeper look at what's really going on in our name and being funded by our taxes.

If we've learned anything over the last couple of decades, we've learned that politicians say and promise one thing, and then months or years later we find that they broke their promises or lied to us in the first place.

All of this seems to me like this is the last desperate efforts of evil, greedy men trying to hold on to power and to keep their corporate house of cards from collapsing. Unfortunately, we live in that house of cards and most of us wouldn't appreciate it collapsing; while on the other hand, the global corporations have interests around the world and will simply move to wherever they can make a profit and be above the law.

When you think about it, it's absurd the amount of secrets that the government keeps from the people. I mean, there really isn't that much that the government really has to do. I'm serious about that. Read The Constitution, the government can only do what they've been empowered (by the people) to do. Subsequently, that's why they've created massive bureaucracies—to justify their existence.

Most people forget that in a democracy, there are no "leaders," only representatives of the people. That's why they call it the House of Representatives, and we elect Senators to represent each state. The President is actually more of an executive secretary in our form of government. We don't have a king or prime minister. That's why we call it the Executive Branch—it's the home of the office workers who do the people's work. Likewise, the Supreme Court is suppose to function as the defenders of The Constitution, and not do the bidding of the political party that put them there (or the corporations that put the politician there in the first place).

This whole system has gotten out of whack. The very same kind of people that the early colonists thought they were fighting against have once again seized control of this country.

All of the spying and secrets and wars and killing—all being done in our name, and with our tax dollars—has made this world a very dangerous place. Which, by the way, further justifies the need for the military to function as a global police force. And believe me, that's no accident either.

Yeah, what they do is scary, mostly illegal and even hard to believe; and yes, it's gotten really out of control. I've included a transcript of The Constitution and Bill of Rights for your perusal.

The Constitution of the United States

We the People of the United States, in Order to form a more perfect Union, establish Justice, insure domestic Tranquility, provide for the common defence, promote the general Welfare, and secure the Blessings of Liberty to ourselves and our Posterity, do ordain and establish this Constitution for the United States of America.

Article. I.

Section. 1.
All legislative Powers herein granted shall be vested in a Congress of the United States, which shall consist of a Senate and House of Representatives.

Section. 2.
The House of Representatives shall be composed of Members chosen every second Year by the People of the several States, and the Electors in each State shall have the Qualifications requisite for Electors of the most numerous Branch of the State Legislature.

No Person shall be a Representative who shall not have attained to the Age of twenty five Years, and been seven Years a Citizen of the United States, and who shall not, when elected, be an Inhabitant of that State in which he shall be chosen.

Representatives and direct Taxes shall be apportioned among the several States which may be included within this Union, according to their respective Numbers, which shall be determined by adding to the whole Number of free Persons, including those bound to Service for a Term of Years, and excluding Indians not taxed, three fifths of all other Persons. The actual Enumeration shall be made within three Years after the first Meeting of the Congress of the United States, and within every subsequent Term of ten Years, in such Manner as they shall by Law direct. The Number of Representatives shall not exceed one for every thirty Thousand, but each State shall have at Least one Representative; and until such enumeration shall be made, the State of New Hampshire shall be entitled to chuse three, Massachusetts eight, Rhode-Island and Providence Plantations one, Connecticut five, New-York six, New Jersey four, Pennsylvania eight, Delaware one, Maryland six, Virginia ten, North Carolina five, South Carolina five, and Georgia three.

When vacancies happen in the Representation from any State, the Executive Authority thereof shall issue Writs of Election to fill such Vacancies.

The House of Representatives shall chuse their Speaker and other Officers; and shall have the sole Power of Impeachment.

Section. 3.
The Senate of the United States shall be composed of two Senators from each State, chosen by the Legislature thereof, for six Years; and each Senator shall have one Vote.

Immediately after they shall be assembled in Consequence of the first Election, they shall be divided as equally as may be into three Classes. The Seats of the Senators of the first Class shall be vacated at the Expiration of the second Year, of the second Class at the Expiration of the fourth Year, and of the third Class at the Expiration of the sixth Year, so that one third may be chosen every second Year; and if Vacancies happen by Resignation, or otherwise, during the Recess of the Legislature of any State, the Executive thereof may make temporary Appointments until the next Meeting of the Legislature, which shall then fill such Vacancies.

No Person shall be a Senator who shall not have attained to the Age of thirty Years, and been nine Years a Citizen of the United States, and who shall not, when elected, be an Inhabitant of that State for which he shall be chosen.

The Vice President of the United States shall be President of the Senate, but shall have no Vote, unless they be equally divided.

The Senate shall chuse their other Officers, and also a President pro tempore, in the Absence of the Vice President, or when he shall exercise the Office of President of the United States.

The Senate shall have the sole Power to try all Impeachments. When sitting for that Purpose, they shall be on Oath or Affirmation. When the President of the United States is tried, the Chief Justice shall preside: And no Person shall be convicted without the Concurrence of two thirds of the Members present.

Judgment in Cases of Impeachment shall not extend further than to removal from Office, and disqualification to hold and enjoy any Office of honor, Trust or Profit under the United States: but the Party convicted shall nevertheless be liable and subject to Indictment, Trial, Judgment and Punishment, according to Law.

Section. 4.
The Times, Places and Manner of holding Elections for Senators and Representatives, shall be prescribed in each State by the Legislature thereof; but the Congress may at any time by Law make or alter such Regulations, except as to the Places of chusing Senators.

The Congress shall assemble at least once in every Year, and such Meeting shall be on the first Monday in December, unless they shall by Law appoint a different Day.

Section. 5.
Each House shall be the Judge of the Elections, Returns and Qualifications of its own Members, and a Majority of each shall constitute a Quorum to do Business; but a smaller Number may adjourn from day to day, and may be authorized to compel the Attendance of absent Members, in such Manner, and under such Penalties as each House may provide.

Each House may determine the Rules of its Proceedings, punish its Members for disorderly Behaviour, and, with the Concurrence of two thirds, expel a Member.

Each House shall keep a Journal of its Proceedings, and from time to time publish the same, excepting such Parts as may in their Judgment require Secrecy; and the Yeas and Nays of the Members of either House on any question shall, at the Desire of one fifth of those Present, be entered on the Journal.

Neither House, during the Session of Congress, shall, without the Consent of the other, adjourn for more than three days, nor to any other Place than that in which the two Houses shall be sitting.

Section. 6.
The Senators and Representatives shall receive a Compensation for their Services, to be ascertained by Law, and paid out of the Treasury of the United States. They shall in all Cases, except Treason, Felony and Breach of the Peace, be privileged from Arrest during their Attendance at the Session of their respective Houses, and in going to and returning from the same; and for any Speech or Debate in either House, they shall not be questioned in any other Place.

No Senator or Representative shall, during the Time for which he was elected, be appointed to any civil Office under the Authority of the United States, which shall have been created, or the Emoluments whereof shall have been encreased during such time; and no Person holding any Office under the United States, shall be a Member of either House during his Continuance in Office.

Section. 7.

All Bills for raising Revenue shall originate in the House of Representatives; but the Senate may propose or concur with Amendments as on other Bills.

Every Bill which shall have passed the House of Representatives and the Senate, shall, before it become a Law, be presented to the President of the United States; If he approve he shall sign it, but if not he shall return it, with his Objections to that House in which it shall have originated, who shall enter the Objections at large on their Journal, and proceed to reconsider it. If after such Reconsideration two thirds of that House shall agree to pass the Bill, it shall be sent, together with the Objections, to the other House, by which it shall likewise be reconsidered, and if approved by two thirds of that House, it shall become a Law. But in all such Cases the Votes of both Houses shall be determined by yeas and Nays, and the Names of the Persons voting for and against the Bill shall be entered on the Journal of each House respectively. If any Bill shall not be returned by the President within ten Days (Sundays excepted) after it shall have been presented to him, the Same shall be a Law, in like Manner as if he had signed it, unless the Congress by their Adjournment prevent its Return, in which Case it shall not be a Law.

Every Order, Resolution, or Vote to which the Concurrence of the Senate and House of Representatives may be necessary (except on a question of Adjournment) shall be presented to the President of the United States; and before the Same shall take Effect, shall be approved by him, or being disapproved by him, shall be repassed by two thirds of the Senate and House of Representatives, according to the Rules and Limitations prescribed in the Case of a Bill.

Section. 8.

The Congress shall have Power To lay and collect Taxes, Duties, Imposts and Excises, to pay the Debts and provide for the common Defence and general Welfare of the United States; but all Duties, Imposts and Excises shall be uniform throughout the United States;

To borrow Money on the credit of the United States;

To regulate Commerce with foreign Nations, and among the several States, and with the Indian Tribes;

To establish an uniform Rule of Naturalization, and uniform Laws on the subject of Bankruptcies throughout the United States;

To coin Money, regulate the Value thereof, and of foreign Coin, and fix the Standard of Weights and Measures;

To provide for the Punishment of counterfeiting the Securities and current Coin of the United States;

To establish Post Offices and post Roads;

To promote the Progress of Science and useful Arts, by securing for limited Times to Authors and Inventors the exclusive Right to their respective Writings and Discoveries;

To constitute Tribunals inferior to the supreme Court;

To define and punish Piracies and Felonies committed on the high Seas, and

Offences against the Law of Nations;

To declare War, grant Letters of Marque and Reprisal, and make Rules concerning Captures on Land and Water;

To raise and support Armies, but no Appropriation of Money to that Use shall be for a longer Term than two Years;

To provide and maintain a Navy;

To make Rules for the Government and Regulation of the land and naval Forces;

To provide for calling forth the Militia to execute the Laws of the Union, suppress Insurrections and repel Invasions;

To provide for organizing, arming, and disciplining, the Militia, and for governing such Part of them as may be employed in the Service of the United States, reserving to the States respectively, the Appointment of the Officers, and the Authority of training the Militia according to the discipline prescribed by Congress;

To exercise exclusive Legislation in all Cases whatsoever, over such District (not exceeding ten Miles square) as may, by Cession of particular States, and the Acceptance of Congress, become the Seat of the Government of the United States, and to exercise like Authority over all Places purchased by the Consent of the Legislature of the State in which the Same shall be, for the Erection of Forts, Magazines, Arsenals, dock-Yards, and other needful Buildings;—And

To make all Laws which shall be necessary and proper for carrying into Execution the foregoing Powers, and all other Powers vested by this Constitution in the Government of the United States, or in any Department or Officer thereof.

Section. 9.
The Migration or Importation of such Persons as any of the States now existing shall think proper to admit, shall not be prohibited by the Congress prior to the Year one thousand eight hundred and eight, but a Tax or duty may be imposed on such Importation, not exceeding ten dollars for each Person.

The Privilege of the Writ of Habeas Corpus shall not be suspended, unless when in Cases of Rebellion or Invasion the public Safety may require it.

No Bill of Attainder or ex post facto Law shall be passed.

No Capitation, or other direct, Tax shall be laid, unless in Proportion to the Census or enumeration herein before directed to be taken.

No Tax or Duty shall be laid on Articles exported from any State.

No Preference shall be given by any Regulation of Commerce or Revenue to the Ports of one State over those of another: nor shall Vessels bound to, or from, one State, be obliged to enter, clear, or pay Duties in another.

No Money shall be drawn from the Treasury, but in Consequence of Appropriations made by Law; and a regular Statement and Account of the Receipts and Expenditures of all public Money shall be published from time to time.

No Title of Nobility shall be granted by the United States: And no Person holding any Office of Profit or Trust under them, shall, without the Consent of the Congress, accept of any present, Emolument, Office, or Title, of any kind whatever, from any King, Prince, or foreign State.

Section. 10.
No State shall enter into any Treaty, Alliance, or Confederation; grant Letters of Marque and Reprisal; coin Money; emit Bills of Credit; make any Thing but gold

and silver Coin a Tender in Payment of Debts; pass any Bill of Attainder, ex post facto Law, or Law impairing the Obligation of Contracts, or grant any Title of Nobility.

No State shall, without the Consent of the Congress, lay any Imposts or Duties on Imports or Exports, except what may be absolutely necessary for executing it's inspection Laws: and the net Produce of all Duties and Imposts, laid by any State on Imports or Exports, shall be for the Use of the Treasury of the United States; and all such Laws shall be subject to the Revision and Controul of the Congress.

No State shall, without the Consent of Congress, lay any Duty of Tonnage, keep Troops, or Ships of War in time of Peace, enter into any Agreement or Compact with another State, or with a foreign Power, or engage in War, unless actually invaded, or in such imminent Danger as will not admit of delay.

Article. II.

Section. 1.
The executive Power shall be vested in a President of the United States of America. He shall hold his Office during the Term of four Years, and, together with the Vice President, chosen for the same Term, be elected, as follows

Each State shall appoint, in such Manner as the Legislature thereof may direct, a Number of Electors, equal to the whole Number of Senators and Representatives to which the State may be entitled in the Congress: but no Senator or Representative, or Person holding an Office of Trust or Profit under the United States, shall be appointed an Elector.

The Electors shall meet in their respective States, and vote by Ballot for two Persons, of whom one at least shall not be an Inhabitant of the same State with themselves. And they shall make a List of all the Persons voted for, and of the Number of Votes for each; which List they shall sign and certify, and transmit sealed to the Seat of the Government of the United States, directed to the President of the Senate. The President of the Senate shall, in the Presence of the Senate and House of Representatives, open all the Certificates, and the Votes shall then be counted. The Person having the greatest Number of Votes shall be the President, if such Number be a Majority of the whole Number of Electors appointed; and if there be more than one who have such Majority, and have an equal Number of Votes, then the House of Representatives shall immediately chuse by Ballot one of them for President; and if no Person have a Majority, then from the five highest on the List the said House shall in like Manner chuse the President. But in chusing the President, the Votes shall be taken by States, the Representation from each State having one Vote; A quorum for this Purpose shall consist of a Member or Members from two thirds of the States, and a Majority of all the States shall be necessary to a Choice. In every Case, after the Choice of the President, the Person having the greatest Number of Votes of the Electors shall be the Vice President. But if there should remain two or more who have equal Votes, the Senate shall chuse from them by Ballot the Vice President.

The Congress may determine the Time of chusing the Electors, and the Day on which they shall give their Votes; which Day shall be the same throughout the United States.

No Person except a natural born Citizen, or a Citizen of the United States, at the time of the Adoption of this Constitution, shall be eligible to the Office of President; neither shall any Person be eligible to that Office who shall not have attained to the Age of thirty five Years, and been fourteen Years a Resident within the United States.

In Case of the Removal of the President from Office, or of his Death, Resignation, or Inability to discharge the Powers and Duties of the said Office, the Same shall devolve on the Vice President, and the Congress may by Law provide for the Case of Removal, Death, Resignation or Inability, both of the President and Vice President, declaring what Officer shall then act as President, and such Officer shall act accordingly, until the Disability be removed, or a President shall be elected.

The President shall, at stated Times, receive for his Services, a Compensation, which shall neither be encreased nor diminished during the Period for which he shall have been elected, and he shall not receive within that Period any other Emolument from the United States, or any of them.

Before he enter on the Execution of his Office, he shall take the following Oath or Affirmation:—"I do solemnly swear (or affirm) that I will faithfully execute the Office of President of the United States, and will to the best of my Ability, preserve, protect and defend the Constitution of the United States."

Section. 2.
The President shall be Commander in Chief of the Army and Navy of the United States, and of the Militia of the several States, when called into the actual Service of the United States; he may require the Opinion, in writing, of the principal Officer in each of the executive Departments, upon any Subject relating to the Duties of their respective Offices, and he shall have Power to grant Reprieves and Pardons for Offences against the United States, except in Cases of Impeachment.

He shall have Power, by and with the Advice and Consent of the Senate, to make Treaties, provided two thirds of the Senators present concur; and he shall nominate, and by and with the Advice and Consent of the Senate, shall appoint Ambassadors, other public Ministers and Consuls, Judges of the supreme Court, and all other Officers of the United States, whose Appointments are not herein otherwise provided for, and which shall be established by Law: but the Congress may by Law vest the Appointment of such inferior Officers, as they think proper, in the President alone, in the Courts of Law, or in the Heads of Departments.

The President shall have Power to fill up all Vacancies that may happen during the Recess of the Senate, by granting Commissions which shall expire at the End of their next Session.

Section. 3.
He shall from time to time give to the Congress Information of the State of the Union, and recommend to their Consideration such Measures as he shall judge necessary and expedient; he may, on extraordinary Occasions, convene both Houses, or either of them, and in Case of Disagreement between them, with Respect to the Time of Adjournment, he may adjourn them to such Time as he shall think proper; he shall receive Ambassadors and other public Ministers; he shall take Care that the Laws be faithfully executed, and shall Commission all the Officers of the United States.

Section. 4.
The President, Vice President and all civil Officers of the United States, shall be removed from Office on Impeachment for, and Conviction of, Treason, Bribery, or other high Crimes and Misdemeanors.

Article III.

Section. 1.
The judicial Power of the United States, shall be vested in one supreme Court, and in such inferior Courts as the Congress may from time to time ordain and establish.

The Judges, both of the supreme and inferior Courts, shall hold their Offices during good Behaviour, and shall, at stated Times, receive for their Services, a Compensation, which shall not be diminished during their Continuance in Office.

Section. 2.

The judicial Power shall extend to all Cases, in Law and Equity, arising under this Constitution, the Laws of the United States, and Treaties made, or which shall be made, under their Authority;—to all Cases affecting Ambassadors, other public Ministers and Consuls;—to all Cases of admiralty and maritime Jurisdiction;—to Controversies to which the United States shall be a Party;—to Controversies between two or more States;— between a State and Citizens of another State,—between Citizens of different States,—between Citizens of the same State claiming Lands under Grants of different States, and between a State, or the Citizens thereof, and foreign States, Citizens or Subjects.

In all Cases affecting Ambassadors, other public Ministers and Consuls, and those in which a State shall be Party, the supreme Court shall have original Jurisdiction. In all the other Cases before mentioned, the supreme Court shall have appellate Jurisdiction, both as to Law and Fact, with such Exceptions, and under such Regulations as the Congress shall make.

The Trial of all Crimes, except in Cases of Impeachment, shall be by Jury; and such Trial shall be held in the State where the said Crimes shall have been committed; but when not committed within any State, the Trial shall be at such Place or Places as the Congress may by Law have directed.

Section. 3.

Treason against the United States, shall consist only in levying War against them, or in adhering to their Enemies, giving them Aid and Comfort. No Person shall be convicted of Treason unless on the Testimony of two Witnesses to the same overt Act, or on Confession in open Court.

The Congress shall have Power to declare the Punishment of Treason, but no Attainder of Treason shall work Corruption of Blood, or Forfeiture except during the Life of the Person attainted.

Article. IV.

Section. 1.

Full Faith and Credit shall be given in each State to the public Acts, Records, and judicial Proceedings of every other State. And the Congress may by general Laws prescribe the Manner in which such Acts, Records and Proceedings shall be proved, and the Effect thereof.

Section. 2.

The Citizens of each State shall be entitled to all Privileges and Immunities of Citizens in the several States.

A Person charged in any State with Treason, Felony, or other Crime, who shall flee from Justice, and be found in another State, shall on Demand of the executive Authority of the State from which he fled, be delivered up, to be removed to the State having Jurisdiction of the Crime.

No Person held to Service or Labour in one State, under the Laws thereof, escaping into another, shall, in Consequence of any Law or Regulation therein, be discharged from such Service or Labour, but shall be delivered up on Claim of the Party to whom such Service or Labour may be due.

Section. 3.

New States may be admitted by the Congress into this Union; but no new State shall be formed or erected within the Jurisdiction of any other State; nor any State be formed by the Junction of two or more States, or Parts of States, without the Consent of the Legislatures of the States concerned as well as of the Congress.

The Congress shall have Power to dispose of and make all needful Rules and Regulations respecting the Territory or other Property belonging to the United States; and nothing in this Constitution shall be so construed as to Prejudice any Claims of the United States, or of any particular State.

Section. 4.

The United States shall guarantee to every State in this Union a Republican Form of Government, and shall protect each of them against Invasion; and on Application of the Legislature, or of the Executive (when the Legislature cannot be convened), against domestic Violence.

Article. V.

The Congress, whenever two thirds of both Houses shall deem it necessary, shall propose Amendments to this Constitution, or, on the Application of the Legislatures of two thirds of the several States, shall call a Convention for proposing Amendments, which, in either Case, shall be valid to all Intents and Purposes, as Part of this Constitution, when ratified by the Legislatures of three fourths of the several States, or by Conventions in three fourths thereof, as the one or the other Mode of Ratification may be proposed by the Congress; Provided that no Amendment which may be made prior to the Year One thousand eight hundred and eight shall in any Manner affect the first and fourth Clauses in the Ninth Section of the first Article; and that no State, without its Consent, shall be deprived of its equal Suffrage in the Senate.

Article. VI.

All Debts contracted and Engagements entered into, before the Adoption of this Constitution, shall be as valid against the United States under this Constitution, as under the Confederation.

This Constitution, and the Laws of the United States which shall be made in Pursuance thereof; and all Treaties made, or which shall be made, under the Authority of the United States, shall be the supreme Law of the Land; and the Judges in every State shall be bound thereby, any Thing in the Constitution or Laws of any State to the Contrary notwithstanding.

The Senators and Representatives before mentioned, and the Members of the several State Legislatures, and all executive and judicial Officers, both of the United States and of the several States, shall be bound by Oath or Affirmation, to support this Constitution; but no religious Test shall ever be required as a Qualification to any Office or public Trust under the United States.

Article. VII.

The Ratification of the Conventions of nine States, shall be sufficient for the Establishment of this Constitution between the States so ratifying the Same.

U.S. National Archives

The Bill of Rights

First Amendment
Congress shall make no law respecting an establishment of religion, or prohibiting the free exercise thereof; or abridging the freedom of speech, or of the press, or the right of the people peaceably to assemble, and to petitition the Government for a redress of grievances.

Second Amendment
A well regulated Militia, being necessary to the security of a free State, the right of the people to keep and bear Arms, shall not be infringed.

Third Amendment
No Soldier shall, in time of peace be quartered in any house, without the consent of the Owner; nor in time of war, but in a manner to be prescribed by law.

Fourth Amendment
The right of the people to be secure in their persons, houses, papers, and effects, against unreasonable searches and seizures, shall not be violated, and no Warrants shall issue, but upon probable cause, supported by Oath or affirmation, and particularly describing the place to be searched, and the persons or things to be seized.

Fifth Amendment
No person shall be held to answer for a capital, or otherwise infamous crime, unless on a presentment or indictment of a Grand Jury, except in cases arising in the land or naval forces, or in the Militia, when in actual service in time of War or public danger; nor shall any person be subject for the same offence to be twice put in jeopardy of life or limb; nor shall be compelled in any criminal case to be a witness against himself; nor be deprived of life, liberty, or property, without due process of law; nor shall private property be taken for public use without just compensation.

Sixth Amendment
In all criminal prosecutions, the accused shall enjoy the right to a speedy and public trial, by an impartial jury of the State and district wherein the crime shall have been committed; which district shall have been previously ascertained by law, and to be informed of the nature and cause of the accusation; to be confronted with the witnesses against him; to have compulsory process for obtaining witnesses in his favor; and to have the assistance of counsel for his defence.

Seventh Amendment
In Suits at common law, where the value in controversy shall exceed twenty dollars, the right of trial by jury shall be preserved, and no fact tried by a jury shall be otherwise reexamined in any Court of the United States, than according to the rules of common law.

Eighth Amendment

Excessive bail shall not be required, nor excessive fines imposed, nor cruel and unusual punishments inflicted.

Ninth Amendment
The enumeration in the Constitution of certain rights shall not be construed to deny or disparage others retained by the people.

Tenth Amendment
The powers not delegated to the United States by the Constitution, nor prohibited by it to the States, are reserved to the States respectively, or to the people.

FOURTH AMENDMENT

THE RIGHT OF THE PEOPLE TO BE SECURE IN THEIR PERSONS, HOUSES, PAPERS, AND EFFECTS, AGAINST UNREASONABLE SEARCHES AND SEIZURES, SHALL NOT BE VIOLATED, AND NO WARRANTS SHALL ISSUE, BUT UPON PROBABLE CAUSE, SUPPORTED BY OATH OR AFFIRMATION, AND PARTICULARLY DESCRIBING THE PLACE TO BE SEARCHED, AND THE PERSONS OR THINGS TO BE SEIZED.

 # THE HOLIDAYS OF OBLIGATION

It was a Sunday; but, because of the long holiday weekend, it felt more like a Monday. "Another holiday," he uttered to himself as he waited for the bartender to bring him a light beer with ice cubes.

He looked around at the mindless patrons in the bar. Some staring at (and hoping to be seen watching) the sports game on the HDTV, others were sneaking a peek at the waitress's exposed skin, but most were just hunched down looking and thumbing their smart phones.

People doing what they're suppose to do, what society dictates, what makes them feel a part of the whole, what might bring them companionship, love, admiration, success, and hopefully sex.

"Is that enough ice?" The bartender inquired as he interrupted the man's people-watching and mental commentary.

"Perfect!" The man replied. "Nothing like an ice cold beer (sips) ahh… now too bad you can't smoke cigars in here."

"Out on the deck," the bartender responded and pointed as he walked away to serve another customer.

A forty-something, fellow with a shaved head and a laptop sits down next to the man and remarks, "I wasn't sure if you'd be here… how's it going? Enjoying the holiday weekend?"

"Holidays… there are too many holidays," the man scoffed. "It's one after the other… There's New Year's Eve followed by MLK, Jr. Day, then there's Super Bowl Sunday, President's Day, Valentine's Day, Fat Tuesday, Saint Patrick's Day, Passover, Easter, Cinco de Mayo, Mother's Day, Memorial Day, Father's Day, Independence Day, Labor Day, Halloween, Veteran's Day, Thanksgiving, Hanukkah, Christmas, Kwanzaa—and those are just the bigger ones. It's a never-ending cycle of holidays… week after week, month after month, year after year. Each one with its own set of rules and things you have to buy—mostly things you have to buy. It's frickin' insane!"

"They can be fun, too," the bald guy replies. "Nothing like getting a day or two off of work!"

"You're missing my point," the man responds. "Sure holidays and days off are great, but it's the consumerism aspect and diversion from reality that I have a problem with."

The man continues… "It's like you don't get a chance to catch your breath, or just live your life anymore—or save any money. If it's not a holiday, it's a sporting event, or an awards show, or a season finale. There's always something… Then there's the natural or man-made disasters on the news… car-chases, shootings, celebrity divorces, the list goes on…

And you know the politicians and Wall Street love it. People are constantly being side-tracked from what's really happening in their towns and country, or what laws are being passed or repealed. Not even the news junkies can keep up with all of the illegal military activities, dirty financial dealings, lobbyists influencing Congressional votes, and a thousand and one other things that would make people's blood boil—if only they knew.

And that's it, we're being kept in the dark by being soothed with holidays, entertainment and sporting events. We've become a society of happy obtuse idiots, just going through the motions of life. Texting, posting, liking and re-tweeting. Sharing our holiday photos and renting movies, TV shows and games.

We do all of this, while the fraudulently-elected (and unelected) people in government, and the corporate criminals in skyscrapers, make life decisions for us behind closed doors. They raise our taxes and lower our retirement and pensions. They allow the cost of medical expenses to continually rise, while wages stagnate. They spend tax dollars to support their lifestyles and interests. Meanwhile, the country's infrastructure is crumbling, our education system is failing, our senior citizens are warehoused in over-priced managed care facilities, and trigger-happy police are becoming more and more militarized—gunning people down in the streets. Our criminal justice system now functions to feed the private corporate prisons with lesser criminals and people who can't pay their bills, while it allows gangs, corporate thugs, and drug lords to make billions of dollars and run our neighborhoods and cities. All of this because they don't want to disrupt the underground economy which accounts for a major chunk of consumer spending and the GDP[1]."

1 GDP, or Gross Domestic Product, is the total dollar value of all goods and services produced in the country. It is used to gauge the size of the economy.

"Man, it sounds like you really thought this through…"

"Not really, I'm just the complete opposite of most people. I don't care about sports or celebrities. I don't get caught up in pop culture or the government propaganda that's spewed out nightly on the network news shows. It's really amazing all of the things you become of aware of when your life's not filled with diversion. But more importantly, everyday I make sure that I take time for living. I look at the world around me. I appreciate nature, the relationships I have. I converse directly with people more than I post or tweet. I get out and walk around at least every other day. I live my life as a personal journey, and don't rely on other people's adventures displayed on a TV or computer screen to replace the act of participating, interacting and doing things myself. Sure, I enjoy a good movie as much as the next person, but it's more fun being the central character in your own story every day."

"I never really looked at it that way…"

"For a long time neither did I. But gradually over time I started to see through the politicians and their speeches, the false advertising, lies and manipulation, and eventually I woke up.

I know it sounds like I'm angry, and there was a time when I was very angry at what was going on; but now, I'm just aware—sometimes even entertained by the absurdity of it all. Of course, it's hard to be entertained by all of the injustice and suffering going on. So I guess mostly I'm just sensitive to things, and make it a point to speak out whenever I can—especially when the bull starts getting really thick."

"Well, I'm due for another beer, how about you?"

"Sure, but I got this one, it's the least I can do for talking your ear off like that."

"Thanks, man."

 **ON RELIGION**

"God has no religion." —Mahatma Gandhi

He flipped through the TV channels... A colorfully-dressed preacher was asking people to send in money; a news anchor was insisting that not all followers of a religion should be blamed for the actions of a few fundamentalists or extremists; and a UFOlogist was making the case that ancient gods were actually alien visitors.

He paused on the latter, lowered the volume, and turned to the woman seated next to him on the sofa and spoke.

> HIM
> The obvious question that I never hear
> anyone ask is, who started all of the old
> religions in the first place?

> HER
> *Looking up from her magazine*
> Wasn't it God?

> HIM
> Which one? Yahweh, Buddha, Krishna,
> Christ, Allah, Brahman, Mazda?

> HER
> Aren't they all the same?

> HIM
> It's true that many of the gods of the
> old religions are similar, or built upon
> the one that preceded them; but others
> are like night and day. Then you have
> all the writings and books and rules on
> how to behave and worship...

HER

Dismissive

It all seems so primitive and silly to me…

HIM

You're right, it is, but still it persists; and
there are new converts each day, with wars
being fought, and more and more people killed
in the name of religion—year after year.

HER

That I could never figure out… You would
think that killing would be a sin, so how
can people kill for a religion?

HIM

A sin in some religions, others not so much.
Hell, look at The Crusades, martyrdom,
or even the so called, War on Terrorism.

HER

But they're all extremists!

HIM

I'm sure many don't see themselves that way.
What seems esoteric to us, is widely accepted
by billions of people. And even though they
won't admit it, followers of one religion feel
they are in direct competition with the others.
That's what the whole missionary thing is
all about, and that's what gaining "the hearts
and minds" is all about—that and oil, of course.

HER

You're talking about government policies,
not religion.

HIM

Don't be so naive to think that government
policies aren't influenced by the religious.

HER

I guess you're right there… It's just that
you'd think that after people flew in planes
above the clouds, and we sent astronauts
into space, people would be over the whole
"heaven in the sky" thing.

HIM

I know… it's like every time physics, biology,
archeology or astronomy disproves some
ancient religious statement, the religions
adapt, alter their interpretation, or are outright
in denial of reality.

Recently the Catholic Church released
a statement saying that the belief in aliens
didn't go against the religion's canon law.

HER

Canon?

HIM

It's a church thing…

HER

So God is an alien then?

HIM

Well, technically, if he, she or it is not from
this planet, they would be considered to
be an extraterrestrial.

HER

I don't know… this whole worshipping and
taking things on faith is too much for me.

HIM

I've given that a lot of thought, and have
come to the conclusion that belief is a
personal thing, and I try not to criticize
other people's beliefs.

Tony Caravan

I've dabbled with Buddhism and a couple
of the "mystical" religions. And I've
experienced some things that could
best be explained as "spiritual" and
going against the accepted laws of physics.

Knowing what I felt, made me more
accepting of what other people may
get out of their religious experiences.

I mean, life's a crazy trip... when you're
a kid, your mind is open to all kinds of
wild imaginary things; but then as you
become more regimented through the
school system and society, imagination
is replaced with conformity and the
concrete material world.

I just think that we'd all be a litte better
off if we kept some of that child
wonder and imagination as we aged.

                    HER
I can't really argue with that... I believe
there are many things in this world that
can't be explained by science. But I
draw the line on blindly following a
religious leader into war or committing
acts of violence.

                    HIM
I totally agree. If only we as a society
could find a way to be more accepting
of other people's beliefs; and at the same
time, find a way to diffuse the violence
between people of different (opposing) religions.
What we really need is a kind of diplomacy
between religious leaders and governments.

                    HER
Amen.

Image of the Virgin of Guadalupe from the fabric Juan Diego gave to the archbishop of Mexico City in 1531

Tony Caravan

THE FIRST AMENDMENT

CONGRESS SHALL MAKE NO LAW RESPECTING AN ESTABLISHMENT OF RELIGION, OR PROHIBITING THE FREE EXERCISE THEREOF; OR ABRIDGING THE FREEDOM OF SPEECH, OR OF THE PRESS, OR THE RIGHT OF THE PEOPLE PEACEABLY TO ASSEMBLE, AND TO PETITITION THE GOVERNMENT FOR A REDRESS OF GRIEVANCES.

# SEDUCED BY POP CULTURE

or, why we ignore what's really going on

I have to admit it, most of my free time is consumed by the audio and visual arts (if you can call them all "art")... I've got thousands of digital tracks, plus three HDTVs and sound systems in as many rooms, a home bar/lounge, and a collection of objects d'art taking up a lot of wall, table, floor and desk space. And believe me, I live a pretty humble existence.

When I'm not listening to music or watching something on a screen, I'm creating, designing or composing my own stuff. In fact, entertainment and pop culture eats into my reading and writing time (and what little real world social life I have left), way more than it should. *Okay, that's me...*

Now when I do read things, or encounter people in the outside world, I find that the majority of people live their lives almost entirely for sports, concerts, television shows, movies, gaming, and of course, tweets, posts, texts and pics on their smart phones. It's 21st Century existence. The by-product of this, unfortunately, is a lack of time being spent paying attention to what's really going on around the world (and here at home).

Aside: I know that some people, who refer to themselves as "news junkies," might argue that they watch CNN, FOX or MSNBC all the time; but I don't consider any of those stations (or the major networks, for that matter) as purveyors of the truth, or reporting what's really going on. In most instances, the mainstream media functions as an outlet for press releases from government and corporate offices.

Spend a week watching Amy Goodman on "Democracy Now" or the Canadian news, BBC World, or English versions of the French or German newscasts on Link TV—it will give you some perspective.

Anyway, this obsession with pop culture has allowed the corporations to seize control of most western governments and re-structure societies to serve their needs and interests. In effect, turning most democracies into plutocracies[1], and widening the gap

---

1 A country or society governed by the wealthy.

between the wealthy and working class to levels not seen since the days of Medieval fiefdoms.

The reason why most people don't see this as such a bad thing, is because they are having too much of a good time watching, listening, tweeting, posting, etc... The old "gilded cage" syndrome. And while there's nothing wrong with getting into the Zen of working and then entertaining oneself; the problem is, the entertaining part is only a temporary thing, and in time, it will become too costly for most people, leaving them with a life of long hours of working, huge debts and servitude to a corporatized government that has no concern for anyone other than their own shareholders or the *crème de la crème* prime consumers.—*You might want to read that run-on sentence once again.*

This state of affairs is no accident of evolution. Rather, it is exactly what the "Powers That Be" have planned for. With the global population increasing exponentially, there are millions and millions of people who are becoming unnecessary to the corporations. Basically, they (the corporations) can survive and flourish indefinitely on a market group that grows at a slower pace than the general population does. This means, they can continue to raise prices and contour their products and services to those who can afford them, and not worry about providing things such as technology, medicine, food, etc. to the "unwashed masses."

I've only painted the broad-strokes here, but I think you get the picture. Basically, this time, WE fiddled while Rome became a stronger empire.

THE GLOBAL POPULATION IS INCREASING EXPONENTIALLY.

THERE ARE MILLIONS AND MILLIONS OF PEOPLE WHO ARE BECOMING UNNECESSARY TO THE CORPORATIONS.

BASICALLY, THE CORPORATIONS CAN SURVIVE AND FLOURISH INDEFINITELY ON A MARKET GROUP THAT GROWS AT A SLOWER PACE THAN THE GENERAL POPULATION DOES.

Tony Caravan

# WHY VERY FEW MANUFACTURING PLANTS EVER NEED TO CLOSE

If a manufacturing plant closes because their profits are down, that usually means that the shareholders aren't getting an increase in quarterly dividends and/or a year-over-year growth in their stock price. It also means that the corporate executives may not be getting as big a bonus from that location.

What it doesn't necessarily mean is that there is anything wrong with the actual business income and expense model or the productivity of the workers, or even the local business climate.

In other words, most factories close because out of the area executives and shareholders aren't making enough to buy another villa, yacht, or pay for another European vacation.

If the disparity of income of workers versus "higher ups" was not as great, plants could operate indefinitely and workers could receive a living raise for as long as there was demand for the products or services produced by the company.

This may sound a little complicated, but it's not. Basically, you have to forget everything you hear on the nightly news and about the stock market going up or down, and just look at the reality on the street. If people are buying the products, then the business is fine. The economics of stock prices and obscene corporate profits has nothing to do with the economics of running a business.

Next time you pass an abandoned factory, think about the day that it closed. The machines still worked, the employees were willing to do their jobs, the roof didn't leak, the lights were on, etc... Actually, the business was probably showing a profit on the products and services being produced at that particular location. The only reason that it probably closed was because some greedy CEO or Veep miles away wanted to make several more millions of dollars, and the profit wasn't high enough for that high of a withdrawal of funds.

This is the reason most businesses leave this country. It's not just about wages, taxes or tariffs (though that is a part of it); it's about exorbitantly high profits for people that, in most cases, are already making billions of dollars.

Some of the richest people in the world (multi-billionaires) are major shareholders in the corporations that produce the products that most Americans consume. I'm talking about the *Fortune* 500 and the *Forbes* billionaires lists. If these aristocrats would take just a fraction less out of their companies, there would easily be enough to pay employees healthcare and provide them with a living wage. The reason why most of them don't do it, has to do with greed—and probably wanting to keep their position on the top 500. Imagine that... a child is under-nourished because some rich bastard in a mansion somewhere is trying to move up a notch on some list of billionaires. *It's pathetic!*

"FORGET EVERYTHING YOU HEAR ON THE NIGHTLY NEWS, AND ABOUT THE STOCK MARKET GOING UP OR DOWN, AND JUST LOOK AT THE REALITY ON THE STREETS."

DIVERSION RULES!

Words and Music by Tony Caravan (BMI)

It's not just the short attention spans, media jingoism,
corporate-funded politicians, and the really scary
behind-the-scenes-stuff-that-nobody-knows-about;
the major obstacle to peace and democracy is diversion.

Never before in the history of civilization have there been so many
diversions for the oppressed.
The gilded cage has become even more plush
with HDTVs, WiFi, smartphones, custom kitchens,
beds, baths and beyond...

As the empire expands and the government becomes a plutocracy,
the people have no idea what's really going on.
In fact, what is reality, is considered fantasy by most.

This current societal condition cannot exist indefinitely.
There are only two possible outcomes:
    1) A total implosion that leads to a totalitarian state; or,
    2) A grassroots movement that rapidly grows to restore
       democracy and sanity.

One or the other will occur in the next few years
the seeds of both are flourishing now.
As far as which one will prevail,
that is a matter of how much of a social consciousness remains.

Song available on iTunes

EYKIW - EVERYTHING YOU KNOW IS WRONG!

Words and Music by Tony Caravan (BMI)

Ah, what do you know?
All you do is sit around and watch the boob tube,
or browse the Internet.
It's clear you're in pretty much of a state of denial about
practically everything.

It's the 21st Century… where most of you look around
trapped in a retro-obsessed culture of pseudo-realities that
change like channels and flow like web pages.

The malady (has) spread in the U.S. in the 1990s
as new communications technologies and the
World Wide Web became ubiquitous.

The puzzling thing about this phenomenon is that
you'd expect a completely opposite result from such
a transformation of the society.

Life's really different in the 2000's compared to the 1990s
In one decade there has been a transmutation from the previous
socio-economic-political natural existence to a
virtual reality world of discontent.
People are going through the motions of life
—diversions to avoid confrontation with reality.

The corporations, politicians and the media
encourage, reward and feed on this behavior
to maintain their wealth, power and property.
Meanwhile the gap between the haves and have-nots
is widening to levels not seen since Medieval England.

The very things that the power elite claim to be doing
or will do if elected have already become so out of reach
to the slave society, that even the dream of achieving them
has become fantasy.

In short, the world has changed and nobody knows it.
EVERYTHING YOU KNOW IS WRONG*!*

The cost of living and the price of the average house
in the U.S. has doubled over the last ten years
but wages haven't.

People have new expenses they never had in the 90s…
Cell phone bills, high-speed Internet bills, computer-related
expenses, high-def, big-screen TVs, higher student loan bills,
higher fuel bills, higher credit card bills, higher health care bills…
You get the picture?
It cost more to live than the average person can earn.
Which makes most people go into debt just to survive.

The majority of people in the U.S. become slaves to the
corporations, politicians and media owners.
There's just nothing to do about it
under this current corporate-capitalist system.

It won't change unless the system is changed
And we know that is very, very unlikely
given the control that the powers that be have now.

In order to keep this slave society going
and the cogs of the machine operating smoothly
the country must find more and more raw materials
to feed the behemoth; unfortunately at the expense of
the people who live on those caches of Earthly treasure.
This inevitably creates blow-back which we've
already tragically seen here.
Again, this foreign policy has persisted for so long
that there's very little chance of change over the
next generation or two.

We're already experiencing problems in the country…
housing, transportation… something's got a pop,
it always does. I just hope it's not my brain,
so I can at least watch the drama unfold.

I'm afraid to report that there are no things we can do;
it's too late: EVERYTHING YOU KNOW IS WRONG!

Song available on iTunes

EVERYTHING YOU KNOW IS WRONG!

THE WORST CHRISTMAS, HANNUKAH, KWANZAA SONG EVER WRITTER OR SUNG

Words and Music by Tony Caravan (BMI)

Santa hats and excessive drinking,
Ugly sweaters and ex-girlfriends,
Candles and crappy gifts,
Bowl games and boring TV specials,
Christmas tunes and very old carols,
Family dinners and arguments,
Fake trees and store-bought treats,
Re-tweets and likes and photoshoped pix
on cards without money and Facebook feeds

Maxing the credit cards to buy presents
for ungrateful bastards who will forget it

Over-crowded soup kitchens and shelters
and society parties for slum lords and the privileged

chorus:
This Christmas, Hanukkah and Kwanzaa
sooth me with prescription drugs and diversion
It's a holiday paradise for the rich and famous
and hell for everyone else who has to live and work and fake it.

Mindless followers barely aware
of what it means to be human
Talking acting, dressing and believing
whatever they're told by the media and politicians

It's predators versus sheep with a ruling class that has parties
and hides behind private armies and domestic spying

repeat chorus

Song available on iTunes

Tony Caravan   101

WARS

"If everyone demanded peace instead of another television set, then there'd be peace." — John Lennon

In 1776 a group of colonists declared independence from England, which sparked the Revolutionary War that lasted until 1783. Some 20 years later, the new United States of America and Great Britain were at it again, in what has become known as the War of 1812 (1812 to 1815). During that entire time there were battles fought in Canada as well as what are now the southern and western territories of the U.S. Elsewhere, on land and sea, there were battles with France, Morocco, Algiers and of course the Native Americans. Subsequently, the first and second Seminole Wars for Florida (ending in 1842); and the Mexican-American War (1846-1848). During and after those wars there were other wars such as the Apache Wars, Third Seminole War, Navajo Wars and Utah War.

In 1861 the War Between the States or Civil War began, which lasted until 1865. What followed were numerous wars with Native Americans leading up to the Spanish-American War in 1898.

In the early 1900s there was the Philippine-American War, Boxer Rebellion, Occupation of Nicaragua, Mexican Revolution, Occupation of Haiti, Occupation of the Dominican Republic—all leading up to World War I (1917-1918). A decade later the United States Stock Market Crash and the Great Depression nearly tore the U.S. apart.

In 1941 World War II began (1941-1945) and ended with the dropping of two nuclear bombs on Japan. The Cold War started a couple years later and continued through 1991. During that time there was the Korean War (or Conflict), Bay of Pigs Invasion, the Vietnam War, Invasion of Grenada, Gulf of Sidra Incident and Invasion of Panama—to name just a few.

In 1990 there was the first Gulf War followed by the Bosnian and Kosovo Wars. The Wars in the Middle East began in 2001 and continue to this day, as does Operation Enduring Freedom, or the War on Terrorism.

Basically, the United States has, more or less, been at war, or involved in wars, since its very beginning.

WAR IS OVER!

IF YOU WANT IT

Happy Christmas from John & Yoko

www.IMAGINEPEACE.com

CIVIL DISOBEDIENCE

"I heartily accept the motto, "That government is best which governs least"; and I should like to see it acted up to more rapidly and systematically. Carried out, it finally amounts to this, which also I believe — "That government is best which governs not at all"; and when men are prepared for it, that will be the kind of government which the will have. Government is at best but an expedient; but most governments are usually, and all governments are sometimes, inexpedient. The objections which have been brought against a standing army, and they are many and weighty, and deserve to prevail, may also at last be brought against a standing government. The standing army is only an arm of the standing government. The government itself, which is only the mode which the people have chosen to execute their will, is equally liable to be abused and perverted before the people can act through it. Witness the present Mexican war, the work of comparatively a few individuals using the standing government as their tool; for in the outset, the people would not have consented to this measure."

from On the Duty of Civil Disobedience
[1849, original title: Resistance to Civil Government]
—Henry David Thoreau

If you replace "Mexican war" in the quote above with Middle East wars, Thoreau is right on—over 135 years later. But that should come as no surprise. Likewise, the 200-year-old quote by Ben Franklin, *"Those who would give up essential Liberty, to purchase a little temporary Safety, deserve neither Liberty nor Safety."* is a sort of slogan for the privacy movement in the U.S.—and rightfully so.

While I'm quoting things, we might as well go way, way back to *The Bible* and Ecclesiastes 1:9 *"What has been will be again, what has been done will be done again; there is nothing new under the sun."* Which I reckon sums it all up.

Great thinkers have been telling it like it is for as long as someone was there to listen and pass down their words. And while there are those in each generation that heed the words of wisdom and experience, most let it pass into one ear and out the other. This is the real tragedy of human existence: not enough of us learn from history—especially those who end up being in charge of things.

Some of the principal people who were responsible for opening my mind were Noam Chomsky, Howard Zinn, Marshall McLuhan, Ralph Nader, Martin Luther King, Jr., Jacque Fresco, Crane Brinton, Bill Moyers, George Carlin, Gore Vidal, and more recently, Chris Hedges. Though over the years there have been countless others who've influence me—including everyone from obscure writers, teachers and filmmakers to friends and family, to people I've encountered on the street or even in a pub.

Anyone, and everyone of us, can make a difference; but we have to be willing to take that first step. For some it may be an act of civil disobedience, or joining a movement—maybe even starting one. For others it may be standing up for your principles or an other person's rights. Sometimes it's just supporting a cause to help right a wrong; or expressing your opinion to the person next to you.

The most important lesson that we can take from history, is that real change only happens when we get involved. And, while there are many great voices out there, and all kinds of people standing on soap boxes shouting, "follow me;" if we just stand idle and watch and wait for some politician or figurehead to get the job done, we'll be greatly disappointed (again).

In this book I believe I've demonstrated how the government does the bidding of the corporations. And, while there are a few politicians out there who are well-intentioned, clearly the system is gamed in favor of the financial interests who really run this county.

That leaves you and me, and all of the other people who see the injustices, inequality and oppression, to do something about it. Which is a pretty tall order, especially when there is so much out there diverting people from reality and causing sensory overload.

We're all bombarded daily with well-crafted half-truths and lies on the corporate-run media, along with endless propaganda and double-speak by politicians, add to that trending tweets and scrolls of posts that encourage us to act in a follow-the-leader mob fashion.

On top of all that, we humans are very adaptable; so even though we may be over-worked and under-paid, we find ways to cope and carve out little moments of fun, contentment and relaxation. And as over-priced as all of the gadgets and services offered to us are, we have come to embrace them and accept that our life consists of hard work followed by a weekend or evening here and there of technological pleasure. After all, it's our reward for being a productive member of society, *right?*

Here is where ideology enters the picture. One group of people are content—even happy—with a life of working for some free time on the weekend and nightly digital entertainment on their TV or hand-held device. While others see modern existence as surreal and fastly becoming a dystopia.

This presents quite a dilemma. On one hand, you've got a government run by corporations that feel it is fine to wage wars, spy on its citizens and kill or imprison anyone who threatens their image of the world—a world that is theirs for the taking. That image also including lavish lifestyles for the one percent made possible by the labors of the 99 percent. Then on the other hand, you have many in the 99 percent category that have become very complacent, and support the wars, killing, violence, inequality and bigotry as necessary for them to "hold on to what they got." And even though they will never be a part of the one percent, they still look up to them, admire them—many even worship them.

That is why the U.S. has a foreign policy of endless wars and empire—it has a lot of support. That, and the fact that the "powers that be" have done a good job of scarring the crap out of a lot of people into believing their safety and lifestyle depends on it.

It's quite a challenge to tell someone sitting in their comfy chair, watching their favorite show on a 72-inch HDTV, holding a can of beer or soda with a delivery pizza in front of them on the coffee table, that they are being deceived and lied to by their government. Chances are, if you did, they'd probably stab you with the American flag pole hanging on their front porch, or shoot you with that NRA-lobbied-for semi-automatic firearm that they have the right to own and carry in their pickup truck.

I'm afraid that those folks are never going to come around. They suffer from cognitive dissonance when it comes to the ideology they've been spoon-fed through the school system, media and pop culture. All we can hope is that, the next generation is more open-minded and perhaps becomes self-aware.

There is, however, an interesting thing about people who are followers, they tend go whichever way the prevailing winds blow. Of course, I'm not saying that this is a good thing; but it is a human nature thing. And it is this is the weakness that the right wing politicians and the media exploit. This is why people are so fast to turn on their neighbors and friends if they see something on the news, or if someone who looks or talks similar to their neighbor is characterized by a bureaucrat as an enemy of the state. But it can also work the other way.

Yes, it's all very complicated. And that's why people of good conscience need to stand up and speak the truth. With so much mental clutter everywhere, and so many diversions, this is one of those pivotal moments in time when clarity of focus is essential.

In a recent op-ed piece in the *New York Times,* Edward Snowden wrote, *"With each court victory, with every change in the law, we demonstrate facts are more convincing than fear."*

What's needed the most right now is for people to show other people that a better way of life is possible. We don't have to be serfs or pawns. We don't have to accept endless wars, militarized police and domestic spying. It is possible to live in peace without having our civil liberties taken away. Just as it's possible to raise the standard of living for all people here and around the world.

Is that idealistic? Sure, and why not? We all know the negatives that we're up against. I propose we focus now on the positives.

"What a Wonderful World[1]" it could be.

Good luck!

---

1 "What a Wonderful World" written by Bob Thiele (as "George Douglas") and George David Weiss. First recorded by Louis Armstrong and released as a single in 1967. Memory Lane Music Group, Carlin Music Corp. and BMG Rights Management

TOO MANY SECRETS.

OTHER TITLES BY THE AUTHOR

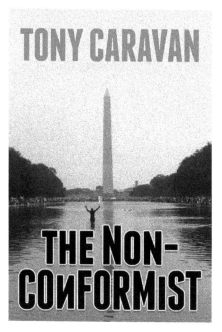

The Non-Conformist

ISBN-13: 978-1500469498

available at bookstores
and online at Amazon.com

also available digitally
on the iTunes bookstore

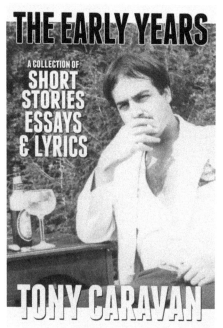

The Early Years

ISBN-13: 978-1496066428

available at bookstores
and online at Amazon.com

also available digitally
on the iTunes bookstore

CPSIA information can be obtained
at www.ICGtesting.com
Printed in the USA
LVHW081510310320
651765LV00008B/136

9 781514 223772